Ghost Tales
OF
America's Haunted Lighthouses

Published by Arcadia Children's Books
A Division of Arcadia Publishing
Charleston, SC
www.arcadiapublishing.com

Copyright © 2025 by Arcadia Children's Books
All rights reserved

Spooky America is a trademark of Arcadia Publishing, Inc.

First published 2025
Manufactured in the United States

Designed by Jessica Nevins
Images used courtesy of Shutterstock.com; p. 62 NOAA Historical Collection/Wikimedia Commons

"Point Loma Lighthouse," previously published in *The Ghostly Tales of San Diego*, by Selena Fragassi, 2022. Copyright 2022 by Arcadia Children's Books. Adapted from *Haunted Heart of San Diego*, by Brian Clune with Bob Davis.

"Port Isabel Lighthouse," previously published in *The Ghostly Tales of the Rio Grande Valley*, by Karen Emily Miller, 2023. Copyright 2023 by Arcadia Children's Books. Adapted from *Ghosts of the Rio Grande Valley*, by David Bowles.

"Can a Lighthouse Outrun its Ghost?" previously published in *The Ghostly Tales of Panama City*, by Patricia Heyer, 2023. Copyright 2023 by Arcadia Children's Books. Adapted from *Haunted Panama City*, by Beverly Nield.

"A Light in the Darkness," previously published in *The Ghostly Tales of St. Augustine and St. Johns County*, by Jessa Dean, 2021. Copyright 2021 by Arcadia Children's Books. Adapted from *Haunted St. Augustine and St. Johns County*, by Elizabeth Randall.

"The Electrified Ghost of the Cape May Lighthouse," "The Camera-Shy Ghost of Absecon," and "Hauntings at Barnegat Light," previously published in *The Ghostly Tales of the Jersey Shore*, by Patricia Heyer, 2023. Copyright 2023 by Patricia Heyer. Adapted from *Haunted Jersey Shore Beaches, Boardwalks and Lighthouses*, by Patricia Heyer.

"The Execution Rocks Lighthouse" and "The Fire Island Lighthouse," previously published in *The Ghostly Tales of Long Island*, by Rachel Kempster Barry, 2020. Copyright 2020 by Arcadia Children's Books. Adapted from *Historic Haunts of Long Island*, by Kerriann Flanagan Brosky.

"The Palatine Light" and "A Rose by Any Other Name . . . Would Still be Haunted," previously published in *The Ghostly Tales of Newport*, by John T. Brennan, 2021. Copyright 2021 by John T. Brennan. Adapted from *Ghosts of Newport*, by John T. Brennan.

"The Nubble Light: Scenic and Spooky," previously published in *The Ghostly Tales of New England*, by Carie Juettner, 2020. Copyright 2020 by Arcadia Children's Books. Adapted from *A Guide to Haunted New England*, by Thomas D'Agostino.

"Fairport Harbor Marine Museum and Lighthouse," previously published in *The Ghostly Tales of Cleveland*, by Beth A. Richards, 2021. Copyright 2021 by Beth A. Richards. Adapted from *Haunted Cleveland*, by Beth A. Richards and Chuck L. Gove.

"South Bass Island Lighthouse," previously published in *The Ghostly Tales of Put-in-Bay*, by Jay Whistler, 2022. Copyright 2022 by Arcadia Children's Books. Adapted from *Haunted Put-in-Bay*, by William G. Krejci.

"Grand Traverse Lighthouse," previously published in *The Ghostly Tales of Michigan's West Coast*, by Diane Telgen, 2020. Copyright 2020 by Arcadia Children's Books. Adapted from *Ghosts and Legends of Michigan's West Coast*, by Amberrose Hammond.

"The Storm-Tossed Specters of Whitefish Point," previously published in *The Ghostly Tales of Michigan's Haunted Lighthouses*, by Diane Telgen, 2021. Copyright 2021 by Arcadia Children's Books. Adapted from *Michigan's Haunted Lighthouses*, by Dianna Higgs Stampfler, 2019.

"Lost Souls of North Shore Lights," "Creepy Tales of the Keweenaw," and "Phantoms of the Ontonagon Lighthouse," previously published in *The Ghostly Tales of Michigan's Upper Peninsula*, by Diane Telgen, 2023. Copyright 2023 by Arcadia Children's Books. Adapted from *Ghosts of Michigan's Upper Peninsula*, by Jennifer Billock.

"Ghosts of the Coast," and "Cape Disappointment and Deadman's Hollow," previously published in *The Ghostly Tales of the Pacific Northwest*, by Deb A. Cuyle, 2022. Copyright 2022 by Arcadia Children's Books. Adapted from *Haunted Graveyard of the Pacific*, by Ira Wesley Kitmacher.

ISBN: 9781467197953
Library of Congress Control Number: 2024949084

Notice: The information in this book is true and complete to the best of our knowledge. It is offered without guarantee on the part of the author or Arcadia Publishing. The author and Arcadia Publishing disclaim all liability in connection with the use of this book.

All rights reserved. No part of this book may be reproduced or transmitted in any form whatsoever without prior written permission from the publisher except in the case of brief quotations embodied in critical articles and reviews.

THE GHOSTLIEST TALES OF AMERICA'S HAUNTED LIGHTHOUSES

A Spooky Anthology

Tillamook, Oregon

San Diego, California

Port Isabel, Texas

TABLE OF CONTENTS & MAP KEY

Welcome to America's Haunted Lighthouses!......3
1. Chapter 1. Point Loma Lighthouse....................7
2. Chapter 2. Port Isabel Lighthouse....................13
3. Chapter 3. Can a Lighthouse Outrun Its Ghosts?..........23
4. Chapter 4. A Light in the Darkness...................29
5. Chapter 5. The Electrified Ghost of Cape May Lighthouse.....35
6. Chapter 6. The Camera-Shy Ghost of Absecon............43
7. Chapter 7. Hauntings at Barnegat Light................53
8. Chapter 8. The Execution Rocks Lighthouse.............63
9. Chapter 9. The Fire Island Lighthouse................69
10. Chapter 10. The Palatine Light.....................77

	Chapter 11. A Rose by Any Other Name... Would Still Be Haunted 87
	Chapter 12. The Nubble Light: Scenic and Spooky........97
	Chapter 13. Fairport Harbor Marine Museum and Lighthouse...101
	Chapter 14. South Bass Island Lighthouse........107
	Chapter 15. Grand Traverse Lighthouse.........115
	Chapter 16. The Storm-Tossed Specters of Whitefish Point....125
	Chapter 17. Lost Souls of North Shore Lights..........135
	Chapter 18. Creepy Tales of the Keweenaw...........145
	Chapter 19. Phantoms of the Ontonagon Lighthouse.......151
	Chapter 20. Ghosts of the Coast..............159
	Chapter 21. A Ghostly Goodbye.............167

Welcome to America's Haunted Lighthouses!

Ahoy, ghost hunters! Are you ready to explore the darkest towers and spookiest lighthouses along our nation's shores? Join us on an epic adventure through storm-swept history, but don't forget your flashlight. These beacons may have been built to save lives, but they've also become home to some of America's most fascinating—and *spine-tingling*—tales!

From windswept Atlantic cliffs to rocky Pacific coastlines, lighthouses have guided sailors through treacherous waters for centuries. But after dark, when storm clouds gather and waves crash below, some towers shine with *more* than just their powerful beams... they also glow with ghostly forms and spectral energy!

In New England, phantom lighthouse keepers still climb worn spiral stairs, faithfully tending flames that went dark decades ago. Along the Great Lakes, the spirits of shipwrecked sailors appear in lighthouse windows, warning others away from dangerous storms. Pacific Coast lighthouses echo with the footsteps of ghostly keepers' children, playing games in the endless twilight. And in the stormy Southeast, Civil War spirits and legendary pirates share haunted watchtowers that have witnessed centuries of maritime history. After all, in America's haunted lighthouses, history isn't just recorded in logbooks—it's lingering in the salty air, whispering on the wind, and waiting for curious visitors just like you to uncover its secrets.

What do you think? Are you brave enough to explore the *ghostliest* towers in America? Read on and follow the ghostly light, if you dare...

CHAPTER 1
San Diego, California

Point Loma Lighthouse

Is there anything more eerie than an abandoned lighthouse that spreads a beacon of illumination across foggy waters? With its bright light shining into the distance, it can almost feel like spirits are walking across the water—and in the case of Point Loma Lighthouse, maybe they are. Located on the western part of San Diego Harbor, it was one of the first lighthouses ever built on California's massive shoreline and it was also one of the tallest ever.

But that presented a big problem. Because it was so high off the ground, when low hanging clouds would come in off the waters and create fog, the light it beamed out was almost completely blocked and it made the lighthouse rather useless in being able to warn ships when they were getting too close to shore. Finally,

after a few decades since it first shone bright in 1855, the lighthouse was taken out of service in 1891.

A new one was built close by but much further down and closer to the water where the light could shine for twenty-five miles and not be blocked by clouds and fog. However, the old Point Loma Lighthouse remained, though it was abandoned, and without a lot of

care it started to fall apart. Former president Woodrow Wilson paid a visit in 1913 and declared the site a historic natural park, which it remains as today. The lighthouse itself is only ever open two days a year, August 25 (the national park's birthday) and November 15 (the day Point Loma was first lit)—but there's still a lot of activity every day of the year.

When people do visit, they might run into Robert D. Israel and his family. Robert was one of the many lighthouse keepers that ran the old Point Loma for eighteen years when it was still fully functioning. His wife and family lived there too—often joining people for picnics on the surrounding land and his kids even had to row a boat across the bay to get to school.

Of course, Robert is no longer alive, but it's said his spirit still lingers in the nooks and crannies of this old building. Sometimes visitors will hear footsteps coming from the upstairs and on the long spiral staircase that reaches up to the watchtower. Some have even said they could feel heavy breathing behind their ears when no one was around. Still others have said they feel like they are being watched or feel cold spots in certain areas of the lighthouse, and a few have claimed to see Robert's actual ghost. It may be he's never really left work and doesn't seem to want to retire anytime soon!

CHAPTER 2

Port Isabel, Texas

Port Isabel Lighthouse

You've been on many car trips with your parents. They love history and nature. You love ghosts. Luckily, everywhere you've gone has something for each of you. So, when you pull up to the Port Isabel Lighthouse, a historic landmark, you figure you're there for *you*. The lighthouse, now a museum, must have lots of ghosts. Spirits from dead sailors and travelers.

Maybe a lighthouse keeper who tripped down the spiral staircase?

Your mom and dad say you are half right. Yes, there will be a paranormal experience, but it won't be inside the lighthouse. You'll have to wait until evening to see it, so your mom suggests you take the museum tour inside while you wait for the dark.

You don't mind. Knowing the story behind the lighthouse might make meeting its ghosts more exciting.

"This lighthouse saved many lives," says the museum guide.

You roll your eyes. You'd hoped this would be more stimulating. Everyone knows lighthouses save lives.

"At night or in storms," the guide continues, "ships

couldn't see the breakers—the rocks along the shore. Many of the ships crashed into the rocks and sunk. So, in the 1800s, a lighthouse was built. It wasn't as big as most. It was only seventy-five steps high, but it lit the bay well enough for ships to sail into port safely."

By this time, you've climbed up to the lighthouse lamp.

"The original light was an oil lamp with three wicks," the guide says. "Now it's a mercury vapor light." The guide points to the green, gold, and chartreuse lights and demonstrates all their flashing patterns. "In 1905, the lighthouse was decommissioned. There wasn't enough water traffic to make it worthwhile. Trains and semitrucks took over most of the shipping traffic."

You yawn. When are you getting to the ghosts?

"That didn't stop the lighthouse from saving lives. Even though ships no longer used it, the lighthouse continued to help. Its angel never stopped coming."

You look around the tower. An angel? *That's* interesting.

"The lighthouse had been a place of safety, not just from storms. During the Mexican–American War, and then the Civil War, soldiers from both sides took refuge here. At times, it was one side who camped at the base, other times, it was the opposite. When cholera and yellow fever hit, the lighthouse became a makeshift hospital." He explains that for generations, people claim to have seen ghostly figures wandering around the lighthouse—often at dusk, after the sun's gone down. "Some people think they might be the ghost of Civil War soldiers. Or the restless spirits of those who died from cholera. People who never received a proper burial."

"What do you think?" you ask.

The guide pauses. "I think there are a lot of things about this place we can't explain."

For a moment, you look up at the lighthouse. You try to imagine all the souls who suffered here, and all the ghosts who likely now call this place home. It's no wonder some of them never left, you think. Maybe all that fear, sadness, and even anger have tied them here.

The guide goes on to say that the first sign there was something supernatural about the lighthouse came after a ship landed safely, even though the seas were rough and the skies black. The sailor in the crow's nest saw a giant angel hovering over the lighthouse. Her glow was so bright, it lit a safe passage through the choppy, dark waters.

The story about the angel spread. According to locals, the angel not only illuminated the night, but it also whispered warnings and advice to those who would listen. A young man claimed he heard the angel telling him to cancel a trip to Mexico City. His fiancée had been looking forward to seeing the city of her ancestors. But he convinced her to change their destination to Acapulco. It was a city in the homeland, too, he argued. The morning after they arrived in Acapulco, they felt their bed move and shake. A massive earthquake had struck Mexico, and over five thousand people in Mexico City died.

The guide leads your group back outside. A light rain is falling. Your mom is ready to get back into the car. "Wait," the guide says. He motions for you to look up. "Watch and you'll understand why people see the angel."

You glance at the sky. As you watch storm

clouds swirl high above, strong winds buffet the lighthouse. They make two windy whirls alongside the top of the tower, gathering droplets of rain as they spin. "*Wow*," you whisper. The sight is mesmerizing. The wind and rain appear to dance together around the lamp, bending the rays of light into what looks like a giant halo that floats above the cupola.

"It looks like angel wings," your dad marvels.

The wind whistles and moans, as if in reply.

For a second, it almost seems like the wind is speaking to *you*.

Mom touches your shoulder. "Let's get back in the car and dry off," she says.

You hesitate. You just heard something you can't explain—you're *certain* of it. The wind, repeating itself over and over, whispers a word that sounds like "*Union*." You look at your parents. They don't seem to have heard it.

Union as in ... Union solider? you wonder. Is this a Civil War ghost trying to talk to you?

You start to open the car door but don't climb in. Then, suddenly, you hear something else, words that are almost lost in the wind. This voice is clear, melodious, and slow. "Don't end up like me."

You crack a puzzled smile. A Civil War ghost with a sense of humor?

The guide was right. The lighthouse *had* saved lives. If not from shining a light in the darkness and keeping countless ships safe, then from its angel. Whether the angel is a paranormal occurrence or a just a weather phenomenon doesn't really matter. Either way, it's nice to imagine that someone—or some*thing*—was looking out for those who come for a visit.

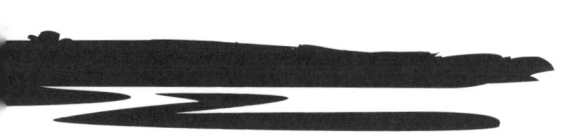

CHAPTER 3
Port St. Joe, Florida

Can a Lighthouse Outrun Its Ghosts?

Cape San Blas juts out into the Gulf of Mexico from the mainland near the port of St. Joe. Built in 1849, the lighthouse guided thousands of ships through the shallow waters found in this part of the Gulf for more than a hundred and fifty years. Without it, ships could not pass safely around the cape. The lighthouse faced many problems because of its location. It was at the mercy of ocean storms, hurricanes, and erosion (the constant wearing away of the shoreline).

A new brick lighthouse had to be built in 1851 because a storm had destroyed the first one. But five years later, the water had reached within eight feet of the door of the new light. Protecting the lighthouse from the Gulf of Mexico was becoming a full-time job.

In 1883, a new ninety-eight-foot metal lighthouse was built farther back from the water. It was made of eight huge cast iron legs, with a watchtower and lantern at the top. A spiral staircase ran up the center. But Mother Nature still had other plans. Storms and ongoing erosion forced the lighthouse to be moved farther inland once again.

Something had to be done. In 2014, the lighthouse on Cape San Blas was taken apart and loaded into trucks. The keeper's house and oil shed were packed onto wide load carriers. A long convoy of trucks and carriers moved the massive tower and the two buildings fourteen miles to the park in St Joe's. It took nearly two days to make the move with thousands watching along the way.

The lighthouse was put back together and then set on a cement base. The keeper's house and the oil shed were then attached to new brick foundations to hold them in place. Within a few days, things were back to normal. The lighthouse beam stretched fourteen miles into the Gulf, once again lighting the way for ships.

Today, the lighthouse rests in St. Joe's at George Core Park, also known as Lighthouse Park. Thousands visit each year, eager to climb the tower and look out over the beautiful white sand beaches.

Workers at the gift shop insist that they have not had any ghostly experiences since the lighthouse moved to St Joe's. But they do admit that people often ask if the lighthouse is haunted.

This might seem a bit strange. When the lighthouse was on the shoreline of Cape San Blas, there were many reports of hauntings and unexplained events. According to local tales, a lighthouse keeper died on duty in 1932. Some say his was a violent death, while others say he died due to hard work and the loneliness of the keeper's job. Others say he died of a broken heart. We will never know.

Soon afterward, there were reports that the old keeper's ghost appeared near the base of the lighthouse whenever bad weather approached. Some claimed to see him climbing the stairs to make certain that the lantern was lit. For some time, people stayed away from the lighthouse because of the feeling of sadness in the air.

Then, just six years later in 1938, the new

lighthouse keeper was murdered. From then on, the area around the base of the lighthouse always felt cold, even in hot weather. Some said that his spirit roamed the grounds looking for his killer.

In the 1950s, a tragic accident at the lighthouse took two more lives. Workers were painting the lighthouse when their safety rope broke. The two men fell to their deaths. Ever since, there have been reports of grayish figures painting the lighthouse in the moonlight. Spookier still, near the anniversary of their deaths, people claimed to hear the sound of piercing screams.

As time goes by, fewer stories are told about the ghosts of the lighthouse. Workers at Lighthouse Park have not reported any ghostly sightings since the move. Perhaps these restless spirits have faded away. Or, could it be that the lighthouse at St. Joe's has outrun its ghosts?

CHAPTER 4
St. Augustine, Florida

A Light in the Darkness

You wouldn't still be reading if you didn't believe in the supernatural, and the St. Augustine Lighthouse is one of the best places in town to experience all things spooky. Now a museum, the lighthouse has many ghostly tales to tell. You might not be able to visit under the light of the full moon—the best time to go—but let's take the 219 stairs to the top and see who we encounter along the way.

Former lighthouse keepers always have the best ghost stories. Since they live and work at the lighthouse, they experience everything. One keeper recalled walking from the tower to the keeper's house one dark night and hearing the crunch of gravel behind him as if someone were following him. But no one was there. He had no shortage of other stories too, including one involving pigeons.

If you know a little about lighthouses, you know that pigeons can be a problem. They're drawn by the warmth of the lights and make their nests inside. You can imagine how gross it can get with pigeons making their home there! So, workers place special blocks to keep them out but still allow the light to escape. But one group of workers encountered more than pigeon poop. While installing these blocks, they looked up and saw a ghostly body hanging front the ceiling!

Tour guides and museum employees will

tell you all kinds of stories. It's up to you to determine if they're real or not. You'll hear of ghostly hands reaching through doors and hearing someone singing when no one is there. Ghost detection equipment is said to light up in certain areas. Chairs have moved around on their own during tours.

The most famous story, though, begins around the time the lighthouse tower was replaced. Beach erosion had taken its toll through the years, and the original coquina lighthouse stood too close to the water. The city officials knew the tower would soon be engulfed by the ocean. A man named Hezekiah Pittee was charged with constructing a new tower—the same striped building you see today. In 1871, Hezekiah brought his family to St. Augustine. He had four children, ranging in age from four to fifteen.

As the lighthouse tower was built, workers used a cement cart to transport construction materials. The cart was about two hundred yards long! It traveled on a rail, so workers could directly unload materials that came in on cargo ships. They then pulled the cart to the construction site to unload. The system used a gate at the water's edge to stop the cart from moving forward.

Construction sites are dangerous places, especially when you have a cart that's double the length of a football field! On July 10, 1873, Hezekiah's kids found out just how dangerous it could be. Along with a ten-year-old friend, they piled into the cart and rode it down to the gate at the water. But the gate didn't stop it. The heavy cement cart flipped, pinning the children under it.

One of the workers managed to rescue Hezekiah's two youngest children, but he couldn't save the others. In spite of the tragedy, Hezekiah finished the job and left with the rest of his family. But the three girls who died that day remained.

People see them frequently, not only at the lighthouse, but also hanging around the neighborhood in their old-fashioned clothes. There's a park with swings across the street, and if you grab a spot, you might find one of the girls swinging next to you. Maybe she'll dare you to swing harder and higher, or maybe she'll just laugh and move on. People see the girls in the lighthouse sometimes too, and they've even tied visitors' shoelaces together as a prank!

After so many years with only each other to play with, the girls are ready for new friends. Maybe they'll let you chase them around the grounds. You'll know they're around even if you can't see them. Listen for their voices in the air, singing, whispering, and giggling. But don't hang out with them too long, or they might just try to keep you with them permanently!

Cape May Lighthouse

CHAPTER 5
Cape May, New Jersey

The Electrified Ghost of Cape May Lighthouse

The beam from the Cape May Lighthouse stretches twenty-five miles out to sea, providing lifesaving information for hundreds of ships that pass along the Atlantic coast. Here on the southern tip of New Jersey, the red-capped lighthouse has guided whaling ships, cargo vessels, and passenger liners through these dangerous waters for more than one hundred-sixty years.

When the Cape May Lighthouse was built in 1859, it was built to last. The Army Corps of Engineers, who built the tower, began by creating a stone platform that reached twelve feet down into the earth. This solid base allowed the lighthouse to withstand the strongest storms and remain intact, despite the weak sandy soil of the area.

Then, to be sure the tower was strong enough to survive hurricanes, they built the tower in two separate layers. The round inside layer is made of brick, which supports the great spiral staircase. The outer layer is shaped like a cone and is made of masonry, which withstands wind, rain, and saltwater spray. On the top, they placed a deep- red twelve-foot cap made of metal and glass. From there, visitors have an amazing view of Cape May, and the overhead flashing beacon can be spotted twenty-five miles out to sea.

Although Cape May Lighthouse is known for being one of New Jersey's most beautiful tourist attractions, it is also known as one of the most haunted lighthouses on the New Jersey shoreline. There are nighttime ghost tours, full moon tower climbs, and even a trolly to carry you to and from the lighthouse. No wonder thousands of people visit the lighthouse each year hoping to meet ghosts!

The many different kinds of ghosts you may meet at the Cape May Lighthouse might surprise you. There are ghosts that try to let visitors know they are present by touching them or making sounds. Other phantoms do not seem to know they are dead, and others repeat the last few minutes of their lives over and over again. There are spirits of the children who once lived there, and even a few ghostly pets of former lighthouse keepers. Within the lighthouse, there are apparitions from the days of the great whaling ships and the shadows of former keepers and their families.

One female spirit dressed in old-time clothing is often seen lugging a bucket of oil up the spiral stairs. Although she climbs the staircase day after day, she never seems to reach the top of the tower. Another ghost hovers on the third landing unable to move upward or downward. There is a weeping phantom surrounded by a group of ghostly children. Sometimes the haunting is replaced by an unruly ghost racing up and down the spiral staircase, searching for something unseen. Spirits of children are heard laughing or seen chasing one another across the grounds. Yet other ghostly toddlers are heard crying, or sometimes reaching out to touch visitors. Many guests report feeling an icy cold chill within the tower, even on the hottest summer day.

One well-known haunting at the lighthouse is that of a former keeper named Samuel Stillwell. Captain Stillwell, an American Civil War hero, served as head keeper at the Cape May Lighthouse for more than twenty-five years. He was in charge in 1891 when a bolt of lightning struck the lighthouse during a thunderstorm. The lightning hit the dome and then traveled down through the tower into the keeper's quarters. The damage was so serious that Keeper Stillwell and his family had to live in temporary quarters for seven months while their home was repaired. Ten years later, lightning once again struck the lighthouse. This time not only were the keeper's quarters damaged but the young daughter of the assistant keeper was seriously burned.

After that, Captain Stillwell kept a constant eye on the weather. Whenever a thunderstorm approached, he immediately evacuated the lighthouse. Just a single clap of thunder would send the no-nonsense keeper into a frenzy, ushering both staff and visitors away from the tower.

Now, many years later, the ghost of Keeper Stillwell appears in the lighthouse whenever a storm comes near. He races up and down the spiral staircase, urging visitors to leave the tower at once. It has been said that he will give a gentle shove to anyone who lingers.

Once he has cleared the tower, Captain Stillwell's ghost keeps staring at the sky. Then, as the storm moves in, he stands outside in the downpour, steering the lightning bolts away from the lighthouse. Some say his ghostly figure can be clearly seen at the *exact* moment the lightning bolt strikes.

The loyal keeper remains there to this day, protecting the lighthouse whenever a storm is near. Captain Stillwell's spirit reminds us that although Cape May Lighthouse is beautiful, it is no place to be during a thunderstorm.

Absecon Lighthouse

CHAPTER 6
Atlantic City, New Jersey

The Camera-Shy Ghost of Absecon

Absecon Lighthouse is not only the tallest lighthouse in New Jersey, but also claims to be the most haunted. Although many people enjoy the view from the 171-foot tower, many others come just to take the daily ghost tours. It seems everyone wants to climb the 220-step spiral staircase to the top of the lighthouse, hoping to meet one of the *dozens* of ghosts that call the tower home.

In fact, there are so many stories of spooky happenings at the Absecon Lighthouse that it is hard to keep count. Eerie voices, unexplained footsteps, and hair-raising screeches are often heard. Doors open and close for no reason. Ghostly figures in torn and frayed uniforms from the American Revolution are seen floating at the base of the tower.

Moaning specters wander from room to room inside the keeper's building in the early morning hours. Inside the tower, ghoulish faces float across the interior walls. Visitors have been frightened by the sight of a single human hand sliding down the handrail of the spiral staircase. As if this were not enough, the smell of cigars can be so strong that workers must turn on fans to clear the air.

Just this summer, it was revealed that one of the best-known ghosts at the lighthouse refuses to be photographed. You might not think a ghost would mind having its picture taken. But in this case, he minded very much.

It was just getting dark when a car with out-of-state license plates pulled into the parking area at the Absecon Lighthouse. The family had planned to arrive in time to climb the tower, but the traffic had been heavy. They could tell the moment they pulled into the lot they were too late. The lighthouse was dark and deserted, with only the "closed" sign visible at the entrance.

Just then the door opened, and a tall lanky tour guide stepped outside. He turned and looked at them, then smiled. At first, they didn't see anything unusual about him. Except for the fact that he was extremely pale, and his clothes appeared to be at least twenty years out of date, he looked like an ordinary tour guide.

When they asked about the lighthouse tour, he looked at his watch and shook his head. "I'm so sorry, the official lighthouse tours end at five o'clock, and it is nearly *six* o'clock." When the younger child began to cry, the tour guide looked as if he might cry as well.

"Well, I could give you a quick tour myself, if you like," he said. "After all, you did drive a long way just to see the lighthouse. Come on, follow me." The grateful parents quickly dug into their wallets, but again, the guide shook his head. "No, money is not accepted on this tour. This is a special nighttime visit," he announced with a giant grin.

They all introduced themselves as they hurried toward the entrance. The guide told them his name was Ambrose but said they could call him "Brosie." The children laughed at his funny nickname, which made the tour guide smile from ear to ear.

He led them to the entrance of the lighthouse tower and then stopped dead in his tracks at the door. He turned around and whispered to the children, "It's after hours, we really shouldn't be here." His eyes sparkled in the dim light as he added," Besides, the tour is *always* more fun in the dark." Before they could answer, he handed each one a small flashlight. "Here," he said. "They are a little dim. These batteries never last long for some reason. But I think they will do."

The family followed the guide into the darkened lighthouse. At first, their flashlights seemed to light the way, but the farther they went into the tower, the fainter the lights became. Brosie never stopped talking. He described how the lighthouse had been built back in 1854, told stories about some of the former keepers, and even shared a ghost story about the famous lighthouse.

Suddenly he shouted, "Follow me!" and bolted up the spiral staircase to the first landing. The family hesitated for a moment, then began their trudge up the steps one at a time. Each time someone stepped on the metal stairs, a dull clanging sound echoed off the walls. After they reached the first landing, the climb seemed easier, although it got darker and colder with every step upward. The children were giggling about the cold, but Brosie didn't seem to notice.

When they finally reached the top of the tower, the

spectacular view made the whole family gasp. On one side, the colorful lights of Atlantic City glittered in the darkness. On the other, it was pitch dark, with only the lighthouse's golden beam shining miles and miles across the inky sea. The view was so mesmerizing that for a long time, no one said a word.

After a bit, the guide said it was time to go, so they began their long trip down the spiral stairs. Their flashlights were useless by then, so they moved slowly and carefully in the dark, everybody feeling for the next step with their foot before they moved farther. They finally reached the bottom, and before they knew it, were back outside.

Brosie said goodbye and was about to leave when the parents asked if they could photograph him with the children. At that, Brosie's smile became a deep frown. He explained that he never permitted anyone to take his picture and turned to walk away.

"*Please?*" the children begged, chasing after him. "Just one picture?"

He sighed as he looked into their pleading faces. "Okay," he agreed. "But just one."

They all gathered together near the base of the lighthouse. Brosie stood in the very middle, with the happy family gathered all around him. The father held out a selfie stick, counted to three, and took the picture. At the exact moment the camera flashed, the tour guide instantly bolted away from them. When they looked up, it was as if Brosie had vanished into thin air.

The family stared at one another. Where had he gone? They scrolled through the phone until they found the picture. There was the family gathered together at the base of the lighthouse, but in the very center where the tour guide had stood...there was only a grayish cloud.

They had met Ambrose, the well-known, camera-shy ghost of Absecon.

Hauntings at Barnegat Light

Ol' Barney, better known as the Barnegat Lighthouse, rests on the northern edge of Long Beach Island, where it stands guard over the dangerous shifting sands of the Atlantic coastline. Since 1859, the 162-foot red-and-white tower has weathered hurricanes, ocean storms, and even an earthquake. It has prevented hundreds of shipwrecks, welcomed millions of people to America, and guarded our shores during two world wars. Barnegat Light is just forty-four miles from the Port of New York, making it an important marker for the thousands of cargo ships that line up to insure safe passage into the harbor each year.

Today, it is one of the most photographed lighthouses in all of New Jersey. Ol' Barney is indeed beautiful, and like many of the other lighthouses along the shore, Barnegat Lighthouse has many stories of hauntings and strange happenings. You won't be able to tell the lighthouse is haunted just by looking at it. After all, it looks like any other well-kept lighthouse. There is a fresh coat of paint on the tower, and the windows are sparkling clean. Inside, there is not so much as a speck of dust, cracked brickwork, or even a cobweb to be found. The state park where the lighthouse stands is well-kept and always filled with happy visitors. But in life (and perhaps, also in death) things are not always as they seem. And sparkling clean though it may be, countless spirits call the old tower their home.

Not everyone who visits Ol' Barney is lucky enough to meet these resident ghosts, but should you be brave enough to climb the 217 steps to the very top of the tower, you just may make a new friend. You might hear the cries of shipwreck victims stranded just offshore, or meet a phantom from the American Revolution.

There are specters of old whaling ships that appear suddenly near the lighthouse, only to vanish right before your eyes. There are noises that can't be explained, and smells so strange they can't be identified. You might meet John Bacon, a spirit not to be messed with, or a pair of sad-looking phantoms searching for their baby. You may be lucky and watch as Andrew Applegate seeks revenge, again and again.

The ghost of John Bacon has been spotted

on Long Beach Island for over two hundred years. His story began in 1780, when the American Revolution was in full swing. The United States had declared independence from Great Britain and was still trying to drive out the British. Battles were being fought all across New Jersey.

One day, a small group of American soldiers managed to capture a British ship when it got stranded on a sandbar not far from shore. On board the ship, they found a large amount of

food and weapons, all of which the American army needed.

They quickly began hauling it onto shore for safekeeping. Although the American soldiers worked without stopping all day, there was still more cargo to bring ashore when it became too dark to work. The men stretched out on the beach to sleep, planning to finish the job in the morning.

It was then that Captain John Bacon and his band of British loyalists came upon the men and killed them as they slept. Although Bacon was captured several months later and hanged for his crime, he swore revenge.

Now it is said that near the anniversary of this grizzly event, the ghostly image of Captain Bacon can be seen storming across the beach swinging a bloody sword at everything in his path. Those who have seen the raging captain flee in terror. (Wouldn't you?!)

Not all ghosts are as bold as Captain Bacon. Some spirits you will hear long before you see them coming. Like the young couple dressed in old-fashioned clothes. If they cross your path in Barnegat Light, the first thing you will notice is a faint jingling sound that grows louder and louder. But the phantoms are not likely to appear unless you happen to be pushing a baby stroller. Only then do they show themselves, pausing for just a moment to peek in at the baby. The jingling then stops, and the couple vanishes right before your eyes.

These specters are from the 1880s, a time when thousands of people fled a great famine in Europe for a new life in America. They hid whatever valuables they had, such as coins, jewelry, or family heirlooms, often sewn into the hems and pockets of their clothes for safekeeping.

One unlucky couple was on their way to America with their newborn baby when an ocean storm wrecked their ship near Barnegat Light. In a panic, they sent their baby to safety on the shore with the first of the rescuers. But while they waited their turn for rescue, a huge wave smashed the ship to pieces. They tried to swim to the beach, but the weight of the valuables in their clothing pulled them to the bottom. They both drowned. Now the spirits of the heartbroken couple can be spotted walking the shoreline near the lighthouse in search of their lost baby, with the sound of coins still jingling in their clothing.

Another tale from Barnegat Light is the

haunting of a former lighthouse keeper. If you wonder if a ghost could ever seek revenge, meet Andrew Applegate. He not only sought revenge during his lifetime but also continues to do it today, nearly a hundred years after his death.

Andrew Applegate may be the most chilling phantom at Barnegat Lighthouse. He was a keeper at Barnegat for many years, so it is not surprising that his spirit is still here. In fact, he died there in 1928, when he got caught in a fishing net and drowned. But the haunting at Barnegat Light by Andrew Applegate doesn't come from the way in which he died... it comes from something that happened four years earlier.

It all started one day in 1924. Andrew was head keeper at Barnegat Lighthouse. He lived there with his wife and family. One day, Andrew was working in the tower when he heard his wife screaming in terror. He raced from the tower to their living quarters, grabbing his shotgun on the way. An intruder had crept into the house and was threatening Mrs. Applegate. Andrew chased the prowler away, firing at him with his shotgun.

Now, on certain nights, Applegate's ghost can be seen once again chasing the intruder. He fires his shotgun at the fleeing figure, then chases him into the dunes. Just when it seems the culprit will escape, the scene suddenly vanishes. Often the scene is repeated two or three times like a mini movie before it vanishes completely.

So, if you visit Ol' Barney, you may be able to watch as Keeper Applegate chases away the intruder. But should you encounter Captain John Bacon and his bloody sword, well, I would *run*.

Execution Rocks Light, Long Island Sound

CHAPTER 8
Mamaroneck, New York

The Execution Rocks Lighthouse

KINGS POINT

Is the Execution Rocks Lighthouse the deadliest lighthouse of all? Located on a dangerously rocky reef a mile north of Sands Point, the abandoned Execution Rocks Lighthouse has a violent history.

What happened here, on these terrible rocks? (Murder.) Do the tormented souls of the murdered continue to visit the site of the rocks and lighthouse? (Quite possibly.)

The most commonly told tales about the Execution Rocks are from the American Revolution. As the legend goes, during the Battle of Long Island, British soldiers rounded up American rebels. They planned to put them to death, but they wanted to do it quietly. They wanted to avoid riling up the American soldiers. Because the British had arrived by ship, they knew very well how to navigate the treacherous waters around Long Island. They also knew of a quiet spot—a rocky island in the middle of Long Island Sound—where they could take the prisoners. Once there, the British soldiers supposedly beat the American rebels and then chained them to the rocks at low tide. As the tide came in slowly and steadily, the prisoners, with no hope of escape, drowned. Many became lunch for hungry sharks. Even worse, the British kept the bodies of the dead soldiers chained to the rocks as a terrifying warning and torment for future prisoners.

As the legend goes, the ghosts of the murdered prisoners haunt the rocks. Some even think they got their revenge when a ship full of British soldiers went down near the rocks, which killed everyone aboard.

With such a terrible history behind it, why did anyone decide to erect a lighthouse atop these deadly, murderous, potentially haunted rocks?

In 1847, under President Lincoln, plans were made to build the lighthouse. The keeper of the lighthouse was to live in the small circular room on the lowest floor, a tiny round space hardly suited for a home. Over the years, the space held several lighthouse keepers before a separate keepers' dwelling was built in 1868.

Once the lighthouse was built, the bad

aura around the deadly place continued. The lighthouse survived two fires: one in 1918 and another in 1921. And in the winter of 1920, a steamer ship called *Maine* ran aground on the rocks due to snow, ice, high winds, and a full-moon tide. Accounts said the ship crashed stern first (the stern is the back of the boat) and nearly hit the lighthouse. Luckily, everyone on board survived, including 14 horses. The bad news? Because the weather was so terrible, it took three long days for the victims of the crash to be rescued. It was brutally cold on board, and there was constant fear that the ship would break apart. Then the lighthouse station's supply of drinking water ran out. For once, the terrible winter weather was helpful—they melted snow to drink and to give to the horses.

Unlike other lighthouses, where keepers stay for decades, it's been said that the average time a lighthouse keeper would stay was only six months. Was it the weather? The tiny living conditions? Or the ghosts? In fact, keepers had an unusual contract: they were allowed to leave their position at any time. As their contract read, "No lighthouse keeper was to ever feel chained to the reef," an eerie reminder of the dark history of the rocks.

Today, the lighthouse has no keeper. It is closed and maintained by the US Coast Guard. But if it ever reopens, would you be brave enough to survive a spell as the keeper of the Execution Rocks Lighthouse?

Fire Island Lighthouse

CHAPTER 9

Fire Island, New York

The Fire Island Lighthouse

Could the Fire Island Lighthouse be haunted? If you ask one of the lighthouse volunteers, they'd probably say no. But rumors of ghosts rumble through the lighthouse's history.

The current Fire Island Lighthouse is actually the second lighthouse to stand on Fire Island. The first lighthouse was built in 1827. For more than 20 years, it served as a guide for transatlantic ships, commercial fishermen, and boaters. Over time, however, the keepers realized that the lighthouse needed to be taller. It also needed to be built from more resilient materials that would stand up to the saltwater and wind.

That new lighthouse was completed in 1858. It stood seven stories high (at 168 feet), and its light was now visible for at least 21 miles. In 1973, the lighthouse was replaced by an electric strobe light. After 150 years serving sailors and seamen, the Fire Island Lighthouse was abandoned. It fell into disrepair and was in danger of being destroyed until it was saved and preserved in 1982 by a group of concerned citizens.

During its years of service, the lighthouse saw its share of history from shipwrecks to hurricanes to pirates. One of the more famous shipwrecks occurred in July 1850 when the captain of the 500-ton ship *Elizabeth* mistook the Fire Island Lighthouse for the Cape May (New Jersey) Lighthouse. The enormous ship violently crashed along the south shore of Long Island, leaving 10 people dead. Among the dead were the famous writer Margaret Fuller, along with her husband and son.

In April 1950, a 432-foot freighter called the SS *Hurricane* hit a sandbar while traveling in the fog. It landed off Fire Island near the

lighthouse. The ship was stranded there for 13 days, and it took tugboats to finally pull it off the beach and back onto the water.

Not all shipwrecks involved such enormous boats. Sometimes, if smaller boats were destroyed in the middle of the night, the lighthouse keeper would wake up to cargo, pieces of ships, and even bodies washed up all along the shore. A haunting way to start the morning off, for sure.

Throughout history, pirates also took advantage of shipwrecks or, even worse, caused them. Pirates were known to light fires on the shores in order to confuse ship captains. The ships would sail toward the light and run aground, and then the pirates would rush aboard to steal all the valuables. Pirates would also keep an eye on the shore, stealing whatever might wash up after a wreck. They were so ruthless, they'd sometimes steal cargo from the rescue ships sent to help damaged boats.

While these true tales of pirates and shipwrecks are haunting, it's the story of a father and his daughter that led some to believe the lighthouse itself is haunted.

Back when the new lighthouse was being built, the lighthouse keeper, his wife, and their daughter were forced to move temporarily into a new home. The lighthouse keeper was very upset about the move because the new home was cold and damp and his daughter was very ill.

As the days went on, the daughter's condition got worse. She developed a fever, and a doctor was called in from the mainland. Back in the 1800s, it wasn't simple to get a doctor out to isolated Fire Island, and the keeper and his wife waited three whole days for the doctor to arrive.

While anxiously waiting, the father climbed up and down and up and down the steps of the lighthouse—182 steps each way—hoping to catch a glimpse of the doctor as he arrived.

Tragically, the doctor didn't arrive in time, and the little girl died. With nowhere to bury her on the rocky shores of Fire Island, the girl was cremated in the fireplace.

Many believe that the clangs and bangs sometimes heard at the lighthouse are the heavy steps of the father walking up and down the steep staircase at night, waiting and waiting and waiting for the doctor who arrived too late.

Bluffs of Block Island

CHAPTER 10
Newport, Rhode Island

The Palatine Light

Pirates don't always come after you on the ocean. Sometimes they wait until you get to shore.

About twelve miles off the coast of Newport sits a small, somewhat porkchop-shaped bit of land called Block Island. It is made up of bluffs, beaches, and the Great Salt Pond. If you like to surf, swim, or build sandcastles, the seventeen miles of Block Island coastline are the perfect place to spend a summer day.

But in the 1730s, the Block Island coastline was a terrible place to spend a winter's night! A tragedy that happened there left a confusing tale of cruelty and murder, courage and sacrifice, and it also left Rhode Island with its most enduring and well-documented ghost story—the Palatine Light!

In 1738, the British ship *Princess Augusta* picked up about 240 emigrants from a region in southern Germany known as the Palatinate. Since the emigrants were called Palatines, their ship became known as the *Palatine*. Captain George Long, his inexperienced crew, and their passengers set sail for Philadelphia in August.

The *Palatine* was a "bad luck" ship from the start. Water supplied for the voyage was contaminated, and soon, half the crew, including Captain Long, and more than half the passengers were dead. The *Palatine* was beset with bad weather and winds that continually pushed it off course. The six-week voyage turned into a sixteen-week ordeal with freezing winter temperatures and vanishing food supplies.

Andrew Brook, the former first mate who now led as captain, tried in vain to land the leaking and creaking ship in New York or Newport instead of Philadelphia, since the winter gales kept pushing them north.

On December 27, during a true New England nor'easter (a winter storm made up of snow, sleet, and wind), the crew spotted what they thought was the Montauk Light coming from the lighthouse on Long Island. They headed for it, but the ship ran aground on the shoals surrounding Block Island.

With the *Palatine* now wrecked and pounded by surf as well as the storm, Captain Brook and his crew abandoned ship and rowed to shore—without their passengers! That's right. They left the remaining Palatines to suffer their fate throughout the long December night.

Now the story splits into several versions. Block Islanders say the crew begged and pleaded with Captain Brook until he finally allowed them to brave the sea and rescue all passengers that remained alive.

According to the crew, Captain Brook bravely faced the storm and rowed to shore to get help. He left the passengers on ship to keep them sheltered and safe. He brought the crew with him in case there was trouble. Block Island had a reputation for harboring "wreckers." (Wreckers were people who robbed victims and looted ships that wrecked on the beach.)

Once Brook felt sure the passengers would be safe, he and his crew rowed back through the waves and rescued all the passengers as well as their belongings. Even after the ship broke up, Brook ordered the crew continue to retrieve cargo until they found all they could.

But there is another account that tells a darker story. In this version, the *Palatine* was lured to the rocks by a false light. Lighthouses were critical in guiding ships to safe harbors and warning them about hidden reefs and dangerous shores. So to light a false lamp and purposefully direct a ship to its doom was a horrible thing to do.

Block Islanders lived a sparse and challenging life while the bustle and wealth of Newport lay just miles across the water. It is documented that Block Islanders were accused of lighting false lights so they could loot the wrecked ships. Ships' captains would go out of their way to avoid the island and those who lived there.

Was it a false light the crew of the *Palatine* saw? Or had months of illness and hunger, bad weather, and bad water caused them to see a beacon that was not there? Regardless, these later accounts also say that while the *Palatine* lay crippled, wreckers from the island descended on it. They looted and plundered the cargo and murdered any survivors who would not join them.

Even though there are various accounts of that evening, there are a few things they all agree on. The *Palatine* was too damaged to repair. To leave it on the rocks was too hazardous to other ships. When the storm subsided, the *Palatine* was towed into deeper water, set on fire, and sunk.

It is also agreed that there was a woman still on the ship who was either forgotten or who refused to leave and abandon her property. As the ship burned, she burned with it, and her screams echoed across the water.

Soon after this tragedy, on dark December nights between Christmas and New Year's Eve, islanders and sailors alike began seeing the ghostly form of a burning ship sail off the coast of Block Island—and with it, they heard the terrified screams of a woman who suffered a horrible fate.

It is said to see the *Palatine* Light is a bad omen. Disaster awaits those who witness it, and tragic storms will soon arrive to wreak havoc. Legend says the *Palatine* Light will continue to burn and haunt Block Island until the pirates, or their descendants, atone for their evil deeds.

Sightings have been recorded since then, including one in 1969. In that sighting, a crowd of people witnessed "a large, glowing fireball" off the coast of the island, near Sandy Point. An investigation revealed no known source for the spectral glow. But believers in the *Palatine* Light know the source.

If you like swimming or shell collecting, hit the sandy beaches of Block Island in the summer. But if you want ghosts, screams in the night, and the phantom shape of a blazing ship on the horizon, take the ferry to Block Island in late December . . . if you dare!

Rose Island Lighthouse

CHAPTER 11
Newport, Rhode Island

A Rose by Any Other Name . . . Would Still Be Haunted

If you know Newport, it comes as no surprise that enemy ships and submarines used to troll the area. The US Navy has been the major employer in and around Newport for over a century.

Founded in 1883, Naval Station Newport is home to the Naval War College, the Naval Justice School, and the Navy's Officer

Candidate School. It is the location of the Naval Undersea Warfare Center and conducts "testing and evaluation of advanced undersea warfare systems" (which probably translates into doing cool secret stuff underwater).

Newport and its famous harbor have been historically important to the US military—particularly the US Navy—from the Revolutionary War to the present day. During World War II, over 80 percent of all the Navy's torpedoes were built in Newport and stored on nearby Rose Island. That's where we'll find our next ghosts.

A mere mile from Naval Station Newport, out in Narragansett Bay, Rose Island is in a good location to support the naval station and defend the harbor. In 1798, the United States took over the island and began building Fort Hamilton. (Yes, named for *that* Hamilton—Alexander.) Work was never completed on the fort, but enough work was done to make it usable for troop training and for quarantining the sick. The fort's walls are over three feet thick, and so during wartime, it became the perfect place to store hundreds of thousands of pounds of explosives. If something went boom in the night, it should stay contained in the fort. But the ghosts that went bump in the night couldn't be contained within the abandoned and crumbling ruins.

During the 1700s and 1800s, Newport was a major center of trade ... and infectious disease. With so many people coming and going from all over the world, the city fell victim to epidemics like smallpox, typhoid, and tuberculosis. To keep Newporters safe, Rose Island became the city's sick ward. Many ill and suffering people were sent to Rose Island. Not so many would leave.

Today, it is reported that lights glow and flash within the fort, although it's not wired with electricity. Doors open and close while no one is there. Faint, muttering voices are heard coming from the quarantine rooms. Are those quiet voices people whispering their final goodbyes? Are the lights those carried by healthcare workers from the past as they check in on the dying? Or are the lights intended as warnings meant to keep the living away?

The poor souls that never made it off Rose Island were buried there. There are no grave markers, but at least two mass graves are known to exist in the island's wooded interior. In 1938, a water tower was built to ensure a freshwater supply to the lighthouse on the island. (The Rose Island Lighthouse went into service in 1870.) Workers constructing the water tower dug up a forgotten military cemetery. The lighthouse keeper at the time, George Bell, reported they found scraps of uniforms, Civil War-era buttons, and human skeletons! But there was work to be done, so the remains and relics were stowed in a large metal box and reburied. Where? No one is sure.

Lighthouse keeping can be lonely, dangerous work, and many lighthouses are reported to be haunted. However, the Rose Island Light is not located in a desolate area. It is not some stark tower set atop cliffs being pummeled by an angry sea. No. The Rose Island Lighthouse looks like a nice family home that just so happens to have a big lamp on the roof. You can go see for yourself, because today you can book a reservation and stay overnight. Want more ghost time? Stay the whole week and walk in the footsteps of Rose Island's former light keepers.

Charles Curtis became an official keeper of the light in 1887 and stuck with the job for thirty-one years, longer than any other Rose Island Lighthouse keeper. He would listen for the "sundown gun" to be fired from Fort Adams, the US Army base across the bay. When he heard it, he would lower the American flag and climb the tower steps to light the lantern for the evening. At midnight, he would climb the tower stairs again and make sure the lantern was still working properly. That is the time when guests staying at the lighthouse hear—and sometimes *see*—his ghost.

Maybe Curtis feels that these guests aren't up to the job of keeping the lighthouse, and so he steps in to help. People who spend the night report that they were woken at midnight by footsteps coming down from the lantern tower and heading to the kitchen (Charles used to stop there every night for a glass of milk) before returning to the tower.

But it's not just footsteps that disturb guests at the Rose Island Lighthouse. Doors open and close with no one there. A figure wearing Curtis's usual baggy pants and suspenders has been seen walking through the keeper's house and along the lighthouse grounds. One guest even seems to have snapped a picture of him. This visitor took a photo of a glass-framed painting hanging in the lighthouse. When he developed it, a chill ran up his spine. There, reflected in the glass, standing just over his shoulder was the unmistakable mustached face of Charles Curtis!

Charles did not tend the lighthouse alone. He shared the island with his family, and it seems that his wife, Christina, might be one of the other documented ghosts. Their grandson Wanton spent much of his boyhood on the island. He came back years later to help with the lighthouse's restoration. Wanton's memories of "how things were" were vital to making the repairs accurate. While there, workers installed an antique kitchen wood stove. When Wanton entered the room, he immediately turned pale. He swore he saw the ghost of his grandmother tending to the stove. No one else saw the ghost, but everyone caught the sudden smell of freshly baked sugar cookies. Now, that's the kind of ghost you might want to keep around!

A Rose by Any Other Name...Would Still Be Haunted

Whether you visit Rose Island for one night or plan to spend the week, get ready for some eerie interactions. Whether it's with the friendly family of light keepers, the disease victims forced into quarantine, or the military members who are buried and reburied here, there will surely be stories you can share when ... or if ... you return to the mainland.

Nubble Light

CHAPTER 12
York, Maine

The Nubble Light: Scenic and Spooky

The Nubble Light in York, Maine, is the most photographed lighthouse in America. When you see it, you understand why. Located on a tiny rocky island less than two hundred feet from Nubble Point, the picturesque Nubble Light stands proudly next to a quaint white house with a pitched red roof and a white picket fence. On a clear day, it sits postcard-perfect between the brilliant blue sky and rich blue waves. The whole scene looks so inviting that it's difficult to imagine the little island having a dreadful and deadly past. But it does.

On Thanksgiving in 1842, years before the Nubble Lighthouse was built, a 396-ton ship called the *Isadore* left Kennebunk, Maine, for New Orleans, Louisiana.

Captain Leander Foss and his crew never made it to their destination.

Less than fifty miles into their journey, a severe storm blew in, ravaging the ship. The next morning, the wrecked remains of the *Isadore* washed up onshore, along with the bodies of Captain Foss and twelve crew members. The only surviving crewman of the ill-fated *Isadore* was Thomas King. The night before the ship set sail, Thomas had a dream that catastrophe awaited on the journey, so he did not board the vessel. He hid in the woods until his crewmates stopped looking for him and departed. Thomas's dream saved his life.

For the rest of the *Isadore* crew, their untimely demise rests heavy on their souls. Witnesses have reported seeing a phantom ship sail past the Nubble Light at night, with a crew of thirteen ghostly sailors staring forlornly out at the sea.

Although the tale of the *Isadore* is not a happy one, there is also a mysterious positive energy swirling around the Nubble Lighthouse. Many people who visit the light feel a comfort and inspiration similar to magic, and some claim that their visit to this beautiful New England landmark changed their lives for the better.

Where does this positive force come from? Maybe it stems from the beauty of the house next to the lighthouse. Or maybe the sense of peace comes from the light itself and the knowledge that, thanks to the Nubble Light, the York shore won't have to see a tragedy like the *Isadore* again.

CHAPTER 13
Fairport Harbor, Ohio

Fairport Harbor Marine Museum and Lighthouse

If you take a thirty-five-minute drive east out of Cleveland, you will find yourself in Fairport Harbor, where the Grand River empties into Lake Erie.

Originally called Grandon, the town was laid out in 1812. The name of the town was changed to Fairport in 1836, and Harbor was added later.

The fifty-five-foot lighthouse was built in 1825 and one of eight lighthouses on the Great Lakes at the time. This lighthouse was not just a beacon for ships on Lake Erie, but also a light of hope and freedom for escaped slaves. The people of Fairport Harbor were abolitionists, and the city became one of the last stops on the Underground Railroad.

The lighthouse was replaced in 1871, and a new sixty-eight foot tower was built.

In 1917, a new lighthouse was built on the west break wall, and in 1925, the original light was extinguished. And in 1945, the Coast Guard turned the lighthouse over to the town.

Toward the end of World War II, there was talk of tearing down the lighthouse, but the town created the Fairport Harbor Historical Society to preserve the town's history and turn the lighthouse into the country's first marine museum.

I know, get to the scary stuff! To understand the ghosts who haunt the lighthouse you need to know who lived here in the beginning. In 1871, Captain Joseph Babcock was named head keeper of the lighthouse, and he brought his family to Fairport Harbor to live there. The family lived in the rooms on the second floor. Mrs. Mary Babcock was a sick woman and had to stay in bed quite a bit, so Captain Babcock gave her some cats to keep her company.

When she passed away, all of her cats seemed to disappear, except for one gray cat. This gray cat, named Sentinel, stayed at the lighthouse for many years, and there are some people who think he never left.

One former curator of the museum, Pam Brent, lived on the second floor for quite a while. She reported seeing a gray cat playing by the kitchen.

However, she didn't have a gray or any color cat! Pam says she has seen the ghostly feline playing throughout the house. One night, he jumped into bed with her—she could feel him lying by her leg but couldn't see him. Many of the museum volunteers and visitors say they have felt a phantom cat rubbing against their legs.

How strange is it the spirit of a cat stayed at the lighthouse all these years? The possible reason became clear when the trustees of the museum decided to have air conditioning installed. A worker had to crawl into a really tight space in the basement and then flip over onto his back. When he flipped over, he felt something under his head. Can you imagine how he felt when he saw the body of a mummified gray cat?

The Fairport Harbor Lighthouse has another spirit besides a ghost cat. People tell stories about a little ghost boy who haunts the lighthouse. While at the top of the lighthouse, people report hearing a little boy laughing. The Babcocks did have a little boy named Robbie, and he died while they lived in the lighthouse. Could the laughing ghost be the spirit of Robbie, a little boy just happy to be at the top of the lighthouse?

If you stop and visit the museum and lighthouse, I hope you're not allergic to ghost cats and you don't mind Robbie keeping you company on your tour. They both just want to make friends with their visitors.

CHAPTER 14
Put-in-Bay, Ohio

South Bass Island Lighthouse

At the far west tip of South Bass Island stands the South Bass Island Lighthouse, erected in 1897. After the end of the Civil War, Lake Erie became a major trade route between the Midwest and the East Coast. Increased ship traffic highlighted a need for safety measures, and because the South Passage between the lighthouses on Green Island and the Marblehead peninsula was especially precarious, the US Lighthouse Board chose Parker's Point as the location for the new lighthouse.

When it was finished, the light could be seen from fifteen miles away, helping guide ships safely through the South Passage. It operated from May until December, when the lake typically froze over for the winter. It required fuel oil to operate, so it had to be attended to daily.

That was the job of the lighthouse keeper, Harry Riley, the first keeper for the South Bass Island Lighthouse. He was there when the lamp was first lit on July 10, 1897. He and his wife lived in the two-and-a-half-story Queen Anne–style brick house attached to the lighthouse.

A year later, Mr. Riley hired an assistant lightkeeper. Sam Anderson moved into the basement of the lighthouse, where he also kept a rather large collection of live snakes. Mr. Anderson didn't keep his job long. About a month after he was hired, the island suffered an outbreak of smallpox. Fortunately, cases were mild, and no one died. But Mr. Anderson became so paranoid, he locked himself in the basement with his snakes. Alcohol seemed to be the only thing to calm his fears. It wasn't long before alcohol took its toll.

On the evening of August 31, 1898, Mr. Anderson emerged from his self-imposed quarantine, raving. Accounts differ about whether he was drunk or whether he'd had a mental health crisis. Regardless, the night would be Mr. Anderson's last. His body was recovered from the lake the next morning.

No records document Mr. Anderson's final

moments. Some people said he tried to sneak past quarantine guards and was brought back to the lighthouse but then threw himself over the cliff rather than be cooped up with the snakes again. Others said he wandered outside the lighthouse all night, howling like a wolf or a dog, and fell to his death. Others swear he emerged from his basement, shouted, "God save them all!" and jumped into the lake.

Whether his death was an accident or suicide will never be known. For Mr. Riley, the tragedy of his friend and coworker's death was more than he could take. The day after Mr. Anderson's death, police arrested Mr. Riley when he was discovered wandering around Sandusky raving about racehorses, then they transferred him to the Toledo Asylum for the Insane.

Doctors at the facility evaluated Mr. Riley and determined he was beyond treatment. A month later, he was dead. There are few details about Mr. Riley's symptoms or diagnosis, and mental healthcare was not as advanced in those days. Treatment usually consisted of institutionalizing anyone who did not exhibit "normal" behavior. People could be institutionalized for reasons such as reading, laziness, tobacco use, religious fervor, or being the victim of domestic abuse. Physical reasons included fever, epilepsy, asthma, smallpox, and swelling of limbs.

Today, modern medicine helps us understand the causes for thousands of physical and emotional illnesses and helps us treat them effectively. But that wasn't the case back in the late 1800s.

We may never know whether the men's conditions were related to their work or whether it was simply coincidence. But one thing is certain: an apparition still wanders the property surrounding the lighthouse. Perhaps Mr. Riley watches over the South Passage, ensuring ships travel safely. Or maybe Mr. Anderson relives the night before his untimely death over and over, as if hoping to change the outcome.

The basement of the lighthouse is another spot for strange phenomena, especially feelings of being watched. Mr. Anderson may have decided the safest place for him to be in the afterlife is in the basement, far from the dangers of smallpox, safe with his snakes. Or maybe the spirits of the snakes still slither along the floor, searching for an escape.

Today, the Ohio State University owns the lighthouse, where there's now a National

Oceanic and Atmospheric Association station monitoring the weather on Lake Erie. Tours are offered during the summer tourist season. Whoever, or whatever, may be roaming the lighthouse and its basement, so be sure to go in the daylight. Unless you're up for a ghostly good time searching for specters!

Grand Traverse Lighthouse

Back in the day, you had to be a very stubborn, determined kind of person to become a lighthouse keeper. You couldn't fall asleep on the job, because a single mistake could lead to disaster on the lake. Is it possible some of these public servants were so devoted to their work that they continued it, even after dying?

Back in the days before GPS and radar, it was hard enough for ships to avoid shoals and shoreline during the daytime. (Shoals are sandbars that make the water shallow.) At night, without a light to help guide them, it was impossible. As ship traffic increased along Lake Michigan in the 1800s, so did the number of lighthouses built along the coast. Without electricity to power them, these lights depended on people to light them, and to keep them going throughout the night. EVERY night.

One of the most important lighthouses along Michigan's west coast is also considered one of the most haunted. Grand Traverse Lighthouse is located on the tip of the Leelenau Peninsula, which sticks out like a little finger near the top of the state's Lower Peninsula. It serves as an important landmark for sailors.

For ships heading southwest, the lighthouse signaled that the relative calm and safety of Grand Traverse Bay was nearby. To ships headed northeast, it signaled they'd better pay attention: the Straits of Mackinac were coming up. This area, which connects Lake Michigan and Lake Huron, is notoriously difficult to navigate. Hidden shoals, winter ice, and sudden fogs have caused shipwrecks to litter the Straits, which are only five miles wide at their narrowest. You can see why having guides along the shore were so important. The U.S. Congress thought so, too. In 1850 they approved funding for a lighthouse on the Grand Traverse site.

The builders spent $4,000.00 of government cash—more than $130,000 in today's money—but they did a horrible job. The first lighthouse was too close to the water, and within five years the foundation had started eroding. The tower could collapse at any time! In 1858, the locals decided to rebuild and do it right.

The new lighthouse was state of the art. The tower dominated the center of the building, with a copper-sheathed roof to protect the light. The lightkeeper's living quarters included four rooms on each of its two stories, with hardwood floors and varnished wooden trim. The extra space meant the keeper could bring his wife and kids to live with him. (And yes, keepers were almost always men. Women only got the post if they took over from a husband or father or brother, after he died or went off to war.)

Although the job was important, it was simple. Every day before dusk, the lightkeeper would climb the stairs to the tower. There he would light a cast-iron lamp fueled by sperm whale oil. (Sperm whale oil gets its name from *spermaceti,* a waxy substance that sperm whales produce in their heads. Before electricity, spermaceti was melted and sold as lamp oil.)

The light would pass through the lighthouse's brand-new Fresnel lens, a complex type of lens that has lots of ridges, like tree rings. These ridges focus and concentrate light into a tight beam, so lots of lighthouses used them. On a clear day, the Grand Traverse light could be seen from twelve miles away. So the keeper had to make sure he never missed a night. Imagine going up those stairs to ignite the light day after day, year after year. You'd be able to do your job in your sleep. Maybe even after you died.

Electricity meant that the days of lighthouse keepers came to end. The Grand Traverse Lighthouse closed in 1972, when it was replaced by an automated light tower nearby. The shuttered building fell into disrepair until 1985, when a local group raised over $1.5 million to preserve this piece of maritime heritage. It opened to the public as a museum the following year. Since then, there have been multiple reports of a ghost haunting the building.

If you walk into the Grand Traverse Lighthouse, you'll see it's pretty small. The tower can only hold four or five people at a time, and you can only reach it by a single staircase. So it's easy to keep track of who is—or isn't—up there. Imagine you're visiting with your family, and you know everyone has left the tower. And yet you hear footsteps on the stairs. Hard-soled shoes walking on the hardwood floors above your head. But *no one is there.*

That's just one ghostly event people have sworn they've witnessed. They know no people are around, but they'll hear voices near the bathroom. They'll feel someone brush past them. Some have even seen the image of a man taking off his shoes, as if relaxing after a hard day's work. These spooky incidents have all happened when *every single living person* in the building was accounted for.

So whose ghost might be haunting the Grand Traverse Lighthouse? Maybe it's Dr. Henry Schetterly, lightkeeper from 1862 to 1873, who actually died in the building. But other people have also breathed their last at the lighthouse. A Coast Guard crewman suffered a heart attack there, while an unnamed woman perished in the kitchen, cause of death unknown. Then there are the last permanent residents of the lighthouse, lightkeeper John Marken and his wife, Bernice. The couple were headed home when they were killed in a car accident on Christmas Eve, 1967.

The ghost doesn't seem to be an angry one. It seems like he—or she—might be one of the lighthouse's most dedicated keepers (or family members). One psychic who visited is sure the mysterious sounds and images come from the ghost of Captain Peter Nelson, who served as lightkeeper from 1874 to 1890 and died in 1892.

Nelson was a former ship's captain—they often retired to keep lighthouses—who was born in Denmark. He started his naval career as a cabin boy, but once in New York City he jumped ship and swim to shore! By his thirties he captained the Great Lakes vessel *Venus*. He later married and had children in his late fifties. So why might he haunt the lighthouse?

A family legend recounts that Peter Nelson was the only one of seven brothers who did not die at sea. Not one, not two, but *all six* of his sailor brothers went to a watery grave. Peter

Nelson, however, was buried on land. Maybe that's why his ghost is restless and haunts the lighthouse where he dedicated many of his final years? Does he seek the water from the afterlife?

Today you can visit the Grand Traverse Lighthouse, which is part of Leelenau State Park. The museum exhibits there don't highlight these ghost stories, but many staff, volunteers, and visitors claim to have seen and heard things that couldn't be explained. Perhaps if you keep your eyes and ears open, you will too.

Whitefish Point Lighthouse

CHAPTER 16
Paradise, Michigan

The Storm-Tossed Specters of Whitefish Point

But now it's time to turn around and sail back toward the Lower Peninsula. Along the way, we'll hit the most dangerous stretch of water in the Great Lakes. For 80 miles, between Munising and Whitefish Point, there's no safe harbor to protect from Lake Superior's deadly storms. Along this "Graveyard of the Great

Lakes," historians say you can find 200 of the 550 ships the lake has claimed.

Whitefish Point juts into Lake Superior just where the lake begins to narrow and approach the St. Marys River. It's so important for navigation that it boasts Superior's oldest operating lighthouse, completed in 1849. It was rebuilt in 1861 with a seventy-six-foot tower, which could be seen by all ships entering the bay from the Soo Locks.

Despite the reliable light marking the shore, there were still other dangers on the lake. In 1853, the *Independence* sank after its boiler exploded. Collisions took the *Comet* in 1875 and the *Osborn* in 1884. The *Isaac M. Scott* and *John B. Cowles* both sank in 1909 after they crashed into each other. A storm swallowed the *Niagara* in 1897.

But the most famous shipwreck along this stretch of water was the iron-ore carrier

Edmund Fitzgerald, which sank with all crew on November 10, 1975. It was memorialized the following year in the number-two hit single "The Wreck of the *Edmund Fitzgerald*."

And these are only some of the lives and ships lost off of Whitefish Point!

With so many tragic losses nearby, it's only natural that ghosts flock to the Whitefish Point Lighthouse. Some people have reported seeing a phantom ship, a gray schooner with full sails, disappearing into nothing. Sailing superstition says that ghost ships like these are doomed to forever reenact their losses on the lake. Perhaps this phantom is the *Invincible*,

the first schooner to be built for Lake Superior shipping—and the first ship to wreck near Whitefish Point, in 1816.

Most of the ghost sightings here have been at the lighthouse and in the crew's quarters, which now has five rooms available for overnight stays. The story of one sighting comes from a guest who visited in 2008. As she slept, a stroking sensation on her face startled her awake. The gentle touch felt like how a parent would caress their child, so she went back to sleep. But at 6:00 a.m., her closed, *locked* door suddenly popped open!

The woman got up and saw no one in the hallway, so she explained it away as air currents. Then she talked to two guests who were staying on another floor. For two days straight, their door had suddenly opened ... *at exactly 6:00 a.m.*!

Not only that, one of them had felt someone

stroking their back in the middle of the night! The other glimpsed the shadowy figure of a man in a blue uniform near their bathroom door. That sure sounds like a ghost to me!

I'd be too scared to investigate Whitefish Point any further, but spooky images and phantom footsteps are just what ghost hunters hope to find. One group braved the haunted lighthouse to set up their video camera. They captured a woman's voice, even though they were the only two people in the building.

The only two *living* people, at least!

Another group of ghost hunters had their own spooky encounters. Their equipment recorded all the classic signs of supernatural activity: weird electromagnetic (EMF) signals, mysteriously drained batteries, and tripped motion sensors. Their thermometers also registered unexplained cold spots, more sure evidence of ghosts.

Nevertheless, they stayed overnight in the crew quarters. That's when one person discovered their pajamas had been *moved* from one end of the bed to the other. I'm sure they didn't sleep very well... especially when the phantoms kept *touching* them during the night!

One psychic visitor claims there are at least fifty spirits haunting Whitefish Point! They include a woman in 1890s dress who stares from the tower out into the lake, a Native American girl who wanders through various buildings, and a young girl in an old-fashioned dress who drifts around—this ghost girl was even caught on tape in an upstairs bedroom. In fact, a staff member recalls sitting on a bed in the crew quarters when she felt a gentle touch on her arm. When she looked over, she found a dented spot on the bed next to her, *exactly the size of a small child*!

So many people have been lost along this stretch of shore that it's hard to figure out who all these ghosts could be. Lifesaving patrols used to find bodies washed ashore after every big storm—sometimes even encased in winter ice! Many of them are buried in unmarked, unrecorded graves.

But the woman in 1890s dress could have been a keeper's wife or someone waiting for a sailor who would never return from the lake. The Native American girl might have been from one of the Anishinabek tribes that dominated the area before Europeans arrived.

(Their descendants, including the Chippewa, or Ojibwa, still live in the Upper Peninsula.) And the little girl ghost? One psychic thinks she was Bertha Endress, the granddaughter of keeper Robert Carlson.

We met the Carlsons at the Marquette Harbor Lighthouse and wondered whether Robert's daughter Cecilia had any connection to the ghost found there. In 1903, the Carlson family moved from Marquette to Whitefish Point, and Cecilia grew up there and got married. But she divorced her husband and later became ill, so her daughter Bertha, born in 1910, often lived at the lighthouse with her grandparents. Bertha eventually worked to help establish the museum there. So perhaps her spirit remains there, continually looking after her childhood home.

On your visit to Whitefish Point, you can tour the Great Lakes Shipwreck Museum and see physical artifacts from the area's many wrecks. And if you dare, stay overnight in the old crew's quarters. Maybe you'll be awoken in the middle of the night by a ghostly touch on your cheek. You might glimpse a phantom ship, sailing through an uncanny mist. When it comes to Lake Superior's dangers, there's no shortage of eerie reminders here!

Good thing we're heading back south. But beware—Michigan's west coast is just as spooky as the rest of the state...

CHAPTER 17
Michigan's Upper Peninsula

Lost Souls of North Shore Lights

To help ships avoid danger, lighthouses dot the Upper Peninsula's coast. In fact, Michigan has more lighthouses—124!—than any other state. That's because it has more freshwater coastline than any state, province, or *country* on the planet. No wonder Michigan took its name from the Algonquian word "mishigamaw," which means "big water"!

Back before electricity, lighthouse keepers

couldn't miss a shift. If you didn't kindle lamps on time, ships might crash—or even sink! Some keepers dedicated years of their lives to their duties.

Some even devoted their *afterlives*. Because ghosts love to haunt lighthouses!

One spooky site stands fourteen miles west of Whitefish Point. Crisp Point Lighthouse started as a lifesaving station in 1876. In 1904, they added a lighthouse tower, nearly sixty feet tall. Over the next sixty years, keepers tried to rescue sailors caught in storms. Often, sadly, all they could do was recover bodies.

One such victim now haunts the property: Three-Fingered Reilly. In November 1919, William Reilly was serving as assistant engineer on the steamer *John Owen*. When a dangerous Lake Superior gale arose, the ship sank with all twenty-two passengers and crew aboard.

Four months later, the Crisp Point keepers

found a body encased in shore ice. While removing it, they accidentally chopped off two of the corpse's fingers. They identified Reilly, but no one came to claim the body. It stayed at the lighthouse, frozen, until the ground could thaw enough for a burial at the station cemetery.

Ever since, visitors to the lighthouse report hearing footsteps trailing them. When they turn around, Three-Fingered Reilly stands there! He often walks the shore, searching for his missing fingers.

Yikes!

He's just one of the ghosts at this lighthouse. The Coast Guard installed automatic lights at Crisp Point in the 1960s, then shut down the whole complex in 1992. Sometime after, three hunters decided to camp in the abandoned keeper's house.

That wasn't very smart.

In the middle of the night, they heard it: thump... *thump*... THUMP!

Thinking someone was coming up the stairs, the young men shouted a warning. When the thumping wouldn't stop, they shot their rifles at the door.

The footsteps stopped, and two of the men went to sleep. But the third stayed awake, just in case. And when the sun rose, he heard more footsteps...

But this time, they headed *down the stairs* and out of the building!

Lighthouse keepers reported for night duty and their shifts ended at dawn. So maybe the men heard a keeper's ghost, working *even after death.*

Whoever haunts Crisp Point Lighthouse has left traces for ghost hunters. When a private group began restoring the lighthouse in the 2010s, they allowed paranormal investigators to visit. Their photos showed nothing but pretty images of the northern lights. But their recordings captured ghostly voices.

"Good afternoon," said one.

"Okay, be silent," whispered another.

"Who are these people?" asked a third.

Jeepers creepers!

If you visit Crisp Point Lighthouse, don't worry. The ghosts will *probably* welcome you.

Just be sure to introduce yourself first.

Grand Island Ghosts

Let's continue west along the UP's northern shore. After seventy miles, we'll reach Grand Island. It sits a half mile north of the city of Munising. Lights dot its thirty miles of rocky coast, protecting boats heading to the shore. One site is notorious—not just for its ghost, but for the unsolved murder that took place there.

The first Grand Island North Light, a forty-foot wooden tower, opened in 1855. Twelve years later, it was replaced with a brick tower and a keeper's house was added. It attracted dedicated workers. Head keeper George Genry looked after the lighthouse for ten years before he and an assistant went missing in 1908.

In late May that year, Genry and Edward Morrison set out for the North Light from Munising. They carried enough supplies to hold them through summer. Genry left his wife in town, promising her he'd write soon.

One week passed without a letter. At first, Mrs. Genry didn't worry; lighthouse keepers stay very busy. But after a second week, reports came in that the North Light remained dark. A search party headed to Grand Island but came back with nothing to report.

The mystery deepened when a sailboat

turned up thirty-five miles away with Morrison's body. It was so badly mangled, they only identified him by his unique star tattoo. But where was Genry? Another trip to the lighthouse found it empty.

Some people said they saw Genry shopping in Munising on June 6, the day before Morrison's body was found. When people checked out the North Light, they found supplies on the dock. They also found recent entries in the lighthouse logbook, and both men left coats on chairs. But no one remained in the building.

The mystery spawned all sorts of rumors. Maybe Genry fell overboard while fishing and then Morrison got caught in a storm. But both men had lots of sailing experience, so some thought murder made more sense. Maybe Genry killed Morrison, threw his body in the sailboat hoping Lake Superior would sink it, and then escaped to Canada.

Morrison once wrote his wife, calling his boss "quarrelsome." He added: "Do not be surprised if you hear of my body being found dead along the shore of Lake Superior."

But in early July, a body washed up by the Grand Island East Channel Light. The keeper there knew Genry and claimed it was him. Although the corpse was never officially identified, a third theory arose: double murder.

Genry had picked up both his and Morrison's paychecks while visiting Munising in June. Perhaps thieves ambushed both men on Grand Island and killed them. Or maybe the island's owner hired someone to murder the lightkeepers because they poached game animals from his land.

The case remains unsolved today. Maybe that's why spooky things happen on the north side of Grand Island. Locals complain that Genry's ghost likes to interfere with anything mechanical. So, if your car stalls or your fridge breaks down, islanders say that's just cranky George Genry, angry that no one's ever brought him justice.

People also say they hear spirits talking along Grand Island's trails. Or shadows move out of the corner of their eye—but when they turn to look, nothing's there! One ghost-hunting team even recorded voices saying the name of one of Grand Island's first settlers!

While the North Light still works today—it was automated in 1961—it's on private land so you can't visit. But you can take a summer trip to enjoy the natural beauty of the Grand Island National Recreational Area.

And if it you hear strange whispers or see a shadow rush by ...

... just tell yourself it's the wind.

CHAPTER 18

Keweenaw Peninsula, Michigan

Creepy Tales of the Keweenaw

We're headed to the northernmost parts of Michigan. First stop: the Keweenaw Peninsula, which juts out like a thumb from the Upper Peninsula.

(That's right, the UP has its own peninsulas, thanks to the Ice Age! First, a mile-thick sheet of heavy ice dug into the ground, shaping the land. Then around twenty thousand years ago, it melted and formed the Great Lakes.)

White settlers first came to Keweenaw in the 1840s to mine copper. Near the tip of the peninsula, they found Eagle Harbor. It provided natural shelter from Lake Superior, but unseen rocks dotted the route leading there. So, they built a lighthouse to help guide ships.

And like many old beacons, Eagle Harbor Lighthouse has its own ghost!

The first wooden structure dates to 1851. Wind and water damaged it, so twenty years later, they rebuilt with a sturdy red-brick tower. To house the keepers and their families, the complex also had a large white house and a smaller brown house.

The Eagle Harbor ghost doesn't welcome people. One Coast Guard officer who lived there in the mid-1970s found it so scary, he asked for a transfer! Here's his story.

Not long after the officer moved into the

lighthouse, he said, "Strange noises would come from the bedroom on the second floor, like furniture was being dragged heavily across the floor, with sounds of loud footsteps." If that wasn't bad enough, lights kept clicking on and off, even when no one was around.

He would open his door to check the light, and it would switch off. But then as soon as he closed his door, FLASH! It would turn on again.

The officer also noticed problems with his alarm clock. It would mysteriously turn off while he was sleeping—or even move from one spot to another!

One visitor to the lighthouse swore she saw a ghost in her bedroom. The man wore a plaid flannel shirt ... but he *had no face*!

When a vacancy came in the large white house on the grounds, the officer grabbed it. But the haunting only got worse! Voices woke him in the middle of the night, and strange noises kept him on edge.

Then there were the creepy footsteps! They started downstairs, echoing off the hardwood floors. "They would then slowly come upstairs, down the hall, and stop at the entrance of the master bedroom. By this time, I would be absolutely terrified."

I would be, too!

Finally, the officer moved to the small brown house and got some peace. But the hauntings haven't stopped, even though the Eagle Harbor Lighthouse is now a historical

museum. One visitor began touring an old bedroom. Suddenly, the cradle there began rocking and shaking, almost coming off the floor!

Sounds like we should get out of here, fast! Maybe it will be more peaceful out on the water...

Ontonagon Lighthouse

CHAPTER 19

Ontonagon, Michigan

Phantoms of the Ontonagon Lighthouse

We're going to head southwest about fifty miles, to the UP's northwest coast. At the Ontonagon Lighthouse, we'll find ghosts created from duty—and disaster.

The first light at Ontonagon was completed in 1853. But like many early Michigan lighthouses, the building couldn't stand up to Great Lakes wind and weather. They replaced it in 1866 with a square, three-story tower attached to a two-story keeper's house.

Tom Stripe became the keeper of the new building of cream-colored brick. But his family remained in town, leaving Tom to care for the property by himself. And this could be a challenge, because Tom had lost his lower right arm in an accident.

Every day, the keeper had one important duty: ensure the lighthouse's oil lamp burned all night. That meant Tom had to carry a five-gallon oil can up the winding staircase. After the lamp switched from using whale oil to cheaper, quicker-burning kerosene, he had to refill it every four hours.

With three stories, that's a LOT of stairs to climb with a heavy load! Still, Tom served as keeper for seventeen years. Because he only had one hand, he often took breaks to rest along the way.

That's why people are sure that Tom's ghost

haunts the Ontonagon lighthouse. The Coast Guard stopped using it in 1963, but now a local historical society runs tours of the lighthouse complex. Tom's old oil can sits on display in the lower hall of the building.

Nighttime visitors to the lighthouse hear the regular clanging of something being set down on the steps. One guide recalled going up the tower on a cold winter evening. Sure enough, she soon heard it...

CLANK. CLANK. CLANK.

When she started back down the stairs, guess what she found?

The oil can had *moved*. Instead of its usual spot downstairs, it rested on the second-floor landing!

Other ghosts like to mess with the displays in the lighthouse. Lamps and furniture will change places overnight. Carefully made beds will look like someone—or some*thing*—has slept in them. Guides also hear voices on stormy nights, warning of Lake Superior's killer gales.

But storms aren't the only danger on the lake...

Ontonagon's Phantom Fires

Even though they are surrounded by water, ships can be destroyed by fire. In the nineteenth century, many ships were made of wood. Or they carried flammable cargo like lumber, oil, or grain.

That's how the *St. Clair* ended up sinking on July 8, 1876. The ship left Ontonagon at midnight with fourteen crew, eighteen passengers, and a load of cattle and feed.

The ship had only sailed about fourteen miles when the crew discovered a fire in the storage hold. In minutes, flames engulfed the ship, making it difficult to launch the lifeboats.

The captain tried to beach the ship so people could swim to shore. But even in July, Superior's chilly waters rarely rise above 50° F (10°C). In the dead of night, only five people survived.

Now every year on July 8, people say the *St. Clair* reappears on the lake as a ghost ship. If you look from Ontonagon Lighthouse to the northeast, you'll see flames flickering on the water, reminding you of twenty-seven lives lost.

The lighthouse hosts ghostly reminders of other ship blazes. In July 1885, the tugboat *Thomas Quayle* sat at its nearby dock. When it caught fire, it quickly burned all the way to the waterline.

Today, people can still see its flames reflected in the lighthouse windows from all the way across the Ontonagon River. And you might think, *That's just a beautiful Lake Superior sunset.* But sunsets don't flicker.

Besides, the river view of the lighthouse faces *east*.

One last fire left echoes at the lighthouse. It raged during the long, hot, dry summer of 1896. Forest fires broke out all over the UP, even in the dried-up swamps near Ontonagon.

On Tuesday, August 25, keeper James Corgan wrote that the wind was "hot and blowing," calling it "a living gale." Flames from the swamp quickly spread to the Diamond Match Company. They had their own sawmill, which had giant piles of sawdust in the yard. The workers couldn't fight the fire, which swept over the factory buildings.

Winds—some gusting up to seventy-five miles per hour—spread the blaze into the town of Ontonagon. Flaming sticks of lumber became missiles, setting buildings alight!

At least one hundred fires burned. Townspeople fled for their lives. The fire killed one person and destroyed 344 buildings, leaving 2,000 people homeless.

At the lighthouse, keeper Corgan, his wife and daughter, and a hired girl worked to save the building. They hauled water from the river up the tower. Then they'd toss it onto the roofs, hoping to douse any sparks. They did this for hours, despite heavy smoke and burning sand.

Finally, the wind shifted. They had saved Ontonagon Lighthouse.

Locals say memories of that fire linger. If you go by the lighthouse when August 25 falls on a Tuesday, keep your eyes open in the evening. As the setting sun casts shadows on the lawn, you'll see them: ghostly figures running up the lighthouse stairs. The shadows haul bucket after bucket to the top before pouring them out on the roof.

If Lake Superior can't protect us from fiery ghosts, maybe we'd better head inland . . .

Ghosts of the Coast

So far, you've read about ghosts galore, by land or by sea. Now, let's head west to the Oregon Coast to see what other spirits await us!

The Ghost in the Lighthouse

Tillamook, Oregon, is known for its cheesemaking, crabbing, and beautiful beaches. It was named in 1891 after a local native tribe that lived in the area. But it is also known for the captivating lighthouse that bears its name, that still stands on a lonely rock out in the ocean, north of the town. Tillamook Rock Lighthouse can be seen from the beach of the Oregon Coast. The lighthouse was going to be built on Tillamook Head, a 15 million-year-old rock, but it would have been too hard and dangerous to construct. Instead, they chose to put the lighthouse nearby on a place simply called the "Rock."

While constructing the lighthouse, bad luck started from day one. The surveyor, Trewavas, fell into the ocean and was never seen again. In 1880, over a dozen men were working on the lighthouse when a violent storm brewed. Everyone thought the men would be killed, but luckily, they survived. A year later, the ship *Lupatia* was sailing in thick fog, veered too close to the Rock, and struck it. *Lupatia* quickly sank to the bottom of the ocean floor and killed all sixteen men aboard. Four of the bodies were swept away by the waves and never found.

A lighthouse keeper named Gibbs was warned the place was haunted. He once saw a ghost ship, but when he called it in, no ship was ever found. It was rumored that the ghost of a former lighthouse keeper was jealous of the new men working there, and he would chase them around and make weird noises. The lighthouse is no longer in use, but it is still haunted!

Cape Disappointment and Deadman's Hollow

Cape Disappointment is a very scenic, coastal state park with cliffs overlooking the ocean, sandy beaches, and tall trees. The area was named by Captain John Meares in 1788, who was trying to find shelter at the opening of the Columbia River but was left "disappointed" when he could not find it, forcing him to move on. The nearby areas earned their names in the year 1853.

The large vessel *Vandalia* came to the area when it became trapped in the cape during a treacherous storm and began to break apart. It

quickly sank to the bottom, taking all twelve men with it. Beard's Hollow earned its name when the body of Captain E.A. Beard, who was in charge of the *Vandalia,* washed ashore a few days later. The bodies of three other sailors were found on another nearby beach, which earned the name Deadman's Hollow. The bodies of the other eight men were never discovered. The wandering souls of all twelve men still linger on the salty shores of the cape.

All of the shipwrecks prompted the building of multiple lighthouses along the coastline. Two lighthouses were built in the vicinity: Cape Disappointment Lighthouse and the

North Head Lighthouse. Today lighthouses are manned by an electronic beacon, but in the old days, men called lighthouse keepers had to live the harsh and lonely life of a keeper. The whipping 120 miles per hour winds and violent storms were extremely frightening and dangerous for the brave men that took these jobs.

One lighthouse keeper named Alexander Pesonen worked the North Head Lighthouse when he fell in love with a beautiful girl named Mary Watson. They married in 1890 and lived at the lighthouse, suffering the storms together. Mary tolerated the life of a lighthouse keeper's wife for 25 long years, but the gloomy weather, lack of outside communication, and harsh living conditions began to wear on Mary. In 1923, she was diagnosed with depression by a doctor in Portland. The next day, she decided to take a walk with her dog, Jerry. When Jerry returned to the lighthouse without Mary, Alexander became very worried!

They found Mary's coat lying in the grass on the bluff that towered 194 feet above the ocean's currents below. On a bank under the cliff lay Mary's corpse. No one knows of Mary accidentally fell or jumped from the cliff. Maybe the lighthouse life drove her to madness.

Her sad spirit has been seen lingering around the lighthouse and its grounds since 1950. Many believe Mary's ghost is looking for her beloved husband, Alexander.

A Ghostly Goodbye

Our exploration of America's haunted lighthouses has come to an end—for now. As we bid farewell, remember that these towering beacons were built to serve as guardians of the coast, their beams cutting through even the darkest night to guide ships to safety. Through howling storms and foggy skies, brave keepers kept their lamps burning bright, saving countless lives at sea. Perhaps that's why so many souls still linger, unwilling—or *unable*—to abandon their posts, even after death.

So the next time you spot a lighthouse on the horizon, listen carefully to the wind and waves. If you should glimpse a ghostly light in the window or hear phantom footsteps on an eerie staircase, don't be afraid. After all, it might just be another "spirited" keeper, faithfully tending their eternal flame.

Discover more of SPOOKY AMERICA—*spine-tingling* tales for kids adapted from our bestselling adult series!

www.arcadiapublishing.com